EMOTIONAL TRANSITIONS
A BOOK OF POETRY

JAMES H. GADDIS

Sistersville, WV
New York, NY

Published by Prospect Press
609 Main Street
Sistersville, West Virginia 26175

Library of Congress Catalog Card Number:
        00-130298

ISBN: 1-892668-21-1

Manufactured in the United States of America

First Edition

10 9 8 7 6 5 4 3 2 1

TABLE OF CONTENTS

✎ IT'S BETTER

It's better to be asked up than to be asked down;
It's better to be asked in than to go around;
It's better to live Godly than try to outwit
One who will never die;
Better moist than dry, better to see stars
* than turbulent skies;*
Better the truth than lies;
Better hellos than good-bys.

🙟 LOVE TRANSCENDS

No boundaries; no shores no time, nor height nor depth:
Love transcends

No color of skin nor ethnicity does love begin;
Love transcends

Through countless gorges of tyranny, from obscurities
to prominence; down through the corridors of time
does love grasp the loneliness of one's heart and there
hope begins; for love transcends

🙟 I NEED TO KNOW

Birds need the air in order to fly,
Fish out of water surely would die.
Flowers need sunshine, mountain tops need the snow;
Crops need rainfall in order to grow;
But most of all, I need to know:

A song needs a melody before it can be played;
A book has a paragraph and then a page;
Stories need morals and poems need to rhyme,
But I need to be with you Lord all the time;
For I need to know that I'm your child.

❧ THE DOOR

The door is often looked upon as an insignificant sight;
But it lets the saints in by day and keeps the thieves out
  at night;
It is where you are greeted and where others bid adieu;
through it enters the cooling breezes of summer
and it keeps winter's cold out too;

It welcomes in the stranger, shakes hands with the
  preacher;
It secures the children and gives comfort to the teacher;
Guard well your post, ye who keep the door;
For it too holds the key to eternity and life for evermore

๛ BEWARE OF THE STRANGER

He might come by day or by night,
he's neither black nor is he white,
just beware, beware of the stranger;
Dressed in silk or maybe cotton,
those who met him have forgotten what
he did to those that dared oppose him;

No face to be seen, to look upon him would
mean that your fate belongs to his pleasure;
Some say he's the light of the ages;
Some say he is the king of kings;
Some say he's Mary's baby;

Just listen to the message that he brings;
Walk softly as you go, speak wisdom to those
you know, the warning of the age is before him;
Don't underestimate the smile upon his face;
Don't be fooled by his embrace; to hug you
might be just to hold you;
Don't mistreat what you don't understand, what
you kill may not be a man, beware, just beware of
*   the stranger.*

SWEET COUNTRY HOME

Sweet country home; I might go away but I won't stay
long; winter's short but summer's long, Lord ain't nothing
like my country home;
City folk love night life and neon signs; but lightning
bugs and moonlight will do just fine, Watchen' ball games
in the dome and sippen' champagne from Rome, won't
take the place of stardust on my face;
Long walks through the wooded symphony, the countries
where the free ought to be;
My pickup's fire engine red and my ladies homebred
and my God has never changed his philosophy.

I WANT TO

I want to Love you, Hold you; Bring you out of the
rain and give you hope again;
I want to console you; remind you; For you I came
to make you smile again;
I want to give you wings to fly away and bring you
to a place of solitude; Lie down beside you and whisper
in your ear, you're never alone for I am always near;
I want to tell you, that I love you, though you left
me you never told me, but I know how much you cried,
it is for you I died.

❧ GOD IS LOVE

God is Love; and Love is God; God is Love and I
   know Love is God;
Love suffers long; love goes on; God is love and I
   know that love is God;
If you feel you can't go on, you are tired of all
   you do; you feel that no one cares and your heart has
   been broken in two; remember God is love and He cares
   just for you; God is Love and Love is of God and He
   will see you through;
So you think you're all alone in this world of hate
   and greed; He blessed this big wide world and He'll
   supply all you need; Remember God is Love and Love
   is eternity; God is Love and Love is God and in Him
   you are free.

ALL I EVER WANTED WAS YOU

*I never wanted fortune and fame; tributes of Glory
and lights around my name; Rhinestones are not
true stones and they fade with time, but you are
that rare jewel that's hard to find; Why settle
for imitations when what's real is in reach;
Why settle for thorns when roses lay at your feet;
To my own self I will be true; for all I ever needed
is you*
    You
        You
            You
All I ever needed was You.

✑ THE MASTER GARDENER

*Eden is a beautiful place; Each plant is a token of
His divine Grace; Streams reflect a rainbow from
heaven, the clouds depict your hair, and as birds
nestle in the trees, praises come from everywhere.*

*Glory to the Most high the universe bows in wonder
at the garden of Earth, how did this occur? I heard
a voice ring out in glee, the Master gardener.*

*Rows of flowers of every kind, a semblance of goodness
so sublime, seeds of virility sown by a dove; offspring's
omnipotence displaying your love;*

*Fruit trees of splendor maple and palm, provide shade
for the weary and balm to keep one calm; Rich pineapple
breaking through the sand, all come from the gardener
with a master plan;*

*We bid all come to this garden for there you will find,
food for the soul nourishment for the troubled mind.
There is no substitute this one I prefer, for this is
the paradise of the Master Gardener.*

❧ HUMANITY

Why must I be white, yellow, or black, called
out of my name by some quirk; categorizing the
masses into subhuman classes; not of unconformity
just a member of humanity;
I'm not a freak of nature nor a metabolical mistake
but a flame glowing in obscurity;
The family of man do I belong not an alien nation;
Not from Mars or Venus or the Apes, I'm a member of
God's creation.

❧ I CAN DREAM

I cannot at will defy time or space;
I cannot fly away on currents of air,
I cannot hide from trouble or despair,
Oh, but I can dream;
I may not be rich, one dare not desire to
be poor, for who would beckon heartaches
of which one must endure;
I cannot escape loneliness and disappointment
from which only God can redeem, I can do none
of these, but I can dream;
I can dream of a new heaven and a new Earth,
I can envision a life full of splendor, I can
conceive a new birth;
Whenever life seems hopeless and I view sunrise
gleam, I am reminded with each new day
comes an opportunity, yes I can dream.

ON ANGEL'S WINGS

On angel's wings I soared the heavens and gazed through
the clouds where I observed a world in turmoil revolving in
  confusion.
I bid the angel stay to rid any delusion, for I could not
  bear what I beheld: hunger, hate, disease, and war.
Then I asked the angel why and he answered with a simple
jest and sighed. They have yet to learn that God knows
best and on His wisdom they must rely for eternity upholds
  His wisdom and we began to cry.
Towering the heavens He showed me Love, hope and
  peace, where Angelic voices filled the air,
On angel's wings we flew away into His loving arms of
  comfort and divine care.

❧ THE MASTER TEACHER

*Teach me maturity and I will grow into a specimen of
your divine will.*

*Teach me placidity and patience will reveal that you are
the master teacher.*

*Teach me how to understand and wisdom will grasp my
hand.*

*Instruct me how to be fearless and courage will not
present me dauntless.*

*Nurture me in Love and my humanness will become
sacred.*

You are the master teacher.

Your instructions are divine.

*In you remains the answer to that mystery which baffles
all of mankind.*

℘ WALK ON

You're not a stranger to pain.
Disappointment wants to be your friend.
It's always raining when you have a parade.
You're always in the sun and not the shade.
Everywhere you go the answer's always no.
But remember the darkest hour is just before day.
I can see the light at the end of the tunnel.
I can hear the crowds cheer.
Keep pushing on in spite of your troubles.
The victory's yours if you persevere.
Walk on, Talk on;
Even if you have to walk alone.
Speak on.
Live on
Sing on.
Pray on.
No matter what they say I know there is a better day.

❧ I'M A SOLDIER

I'm a soldier, In the Army of the Lord.
I'm a soldier, in the Army.
I'm a soldier, in the Army of the Lord. I'm a soldier.
In the Army.
Left right. Join fight.
Serve the Lord with all your might.
Don't give up and don't give in.
For there's soul, He's sure to win.
Cause
I'm a soldier. In the Army of the Lord.
I'm a soldier. In the Army.
Put your hands to the plow and don't allow the things
*   of this world to get you down.*
Wear a smile and not a frown.
Twelve men turned this world upside down.
Cause
You're a soldier. In the Army of the Lord.
You're a soldier. In the Army.

❧ TRANSFORMATION

Only God know the essence of one's life. God gave us life for a purpose.

The deceased has served his purpose. He lived a fruitful life. In order to pass from one stage to another one must be changed. Therefore death is a certain phenomenon.

Christ died that we might live.
He conquered death on the cross.

Death is a certain occurrence. Just as sure as one is born one will die.

Lord, make me to know mine end, and the measure of my days, what it is; that I may know how frail I am. Life is so uncertain.

We live we die; We prosper; We fail but the culmination of our existence depends upon our relationship with God.

But know of a certainty, with Christ we will be transformed.

We will be changed from mortal to immortal. We will shed this mortal body and put on an immortal one.

❧ PAIN

The depth of one's sorrow
cannot be measured by
behavior alone.
Mental suffering is a struggle
that begins with the conception
cognizance; it begins with
the battle of taboos and mores.
Hurt rides the waves of
consciousness; it peaks
on the hilltops of despair.
But God sends the rays
of love to heal the
wounded soul that has
been battered by disappointment
breathes upon that wound with
the breath of His Spirit and
Pain strengthens
Pain sensitizes
Pain gives depth.

YOU'RE MY FATHER

I'm amazed at all you do.
For all the things that come from you.
The birds and the trees, the flowers and bees.
I know you'll see us through,
because of what you say and do,
The Earth and galaxies, the oceans and the seas.
You're my Father. You're my Father.
To know you is to love You.
To fear you is wise.
For who can calm the raging seas and open blinded eyes.
You came as a baby engulfed in love.
Love that comes only from above.
You came as a man engulfed in poverty you bore
all our pain;
You died only to rise again.
You are my Father.
You are my Father.

I AM

*I am indigent, I am heart broken, my spirit has
been wounded; I have been humbled by my tragedies;
I have been uplifted by my triumphs;
Maturity has surrounded childness; Manhood has
evolved from adversity;
To mourn is human; Sorrow is a seed planted in
tribulation that will blossom into jubilation;
The spirit will not resign itself to despair;
Deep within the eternal soul lies the dormant giant
of victory that will overcome all obstacles;
Oh how I rejoice in knowing that victory has arrived.
It is secured in the eternal halls of justice;
My wounds have healed; my heart is mended. My
spirit has been revived.*

ODE TO A SLAVE

*Jumping higher but never leaving the ground;
Running faster but never leaving the starting line.
Seeing farther yet I'm blind; Ode to an enclave; I'm
a slave; Building houses and dwelling in caves; life
lines for victims but I cannot be saved; antidotes
for those who were destined for the grave; I died
for lack of the redress, I'm just a slave;
There is a bright side to this tale; for the blind
there is Braille; For those who toil they will
eventually prevail; For those who run there is
a finish line; There is freedom in the grave;
There is liberty for the slave.*

❧ I AM BLACK BUT COMELY

*I am black but comely, Look not upon me because I am
black nor negatively react to me because of genetics,
the cruelty of nature as well as the insensitivity of an
indifferent society.*

*Look upon me as I look upon myself and that is with
great anticipation. Within me lies the hope of the
world. The corridors of science, medicine, space, and
the Word of God which defines the human race awaits
the grip of my hand. Look not upon me because I'm
black but try to understand, because my feet defied
racism in the race for humanity; I ran like the wind.
Again I prolonged life with blood plasma but I died for
lack of it. When you stop at a traffic light think of me.*

*I am black but comely. From the simple peanut my
imagination allowed me to make a contribution to the
world. I have soared the air in airplanes, sailed the
seas in ships. I help to set many a captive free. But
most of all it was my design that laid the foundation
for Washington D.C.*

*Spat upon and beaten for the right to be free, I stand
tall as the descendants of slaves in a forest of tyranny;
I am black but comely no more nor less. Respect my
right to live. Don't be afraid of my face for despite its
color I'm a part of the human race.*

❧ SLAVERY AND PROSE
PAUL LAURANCE DUNBAR

The son of a runaway slave I inherited the genes of freedom.

Chains could not bid the lines of rhyme that tell of those awesome days.

My father ran away that I might one day say that men born free must forever be on guard for the beast of slavery.

I speak of that dismal ship whose bowels bore broken spirits of those who once stood tall as drums beckoned the call of mighty warrior's who conquered all that opposed them.

I end this prose with history's advice. Those who might give themselves to drink and vice listen to these words and think twice. In order to fight you must learn to think, read and write in order to stay the adversary at midnight.

❧ THE OLD MAN'S PAIN

Wrinkles now prevail his hard dark skin that once shined as the dark velvet canvas of midnight. His dark brown eyes shined like stars on a moonlight night and his towering forehead stood out like California pines.

Now torn from the harsh elements of slavery, his lips trembling from tobacco stains I shutter as I think of the old man's pain.

Feet that once caused him to stride like a deer in full stride now seem to buckle from the harshness of the sweltering heat hoeing mile long rows of cotton in the blistering Mississippi sun.

The myth of amber waves of grain; tears, grief from promises not kept, I try to imagine the old man's pain.
His back bowed toward the Earth from the weight of slavery he bore his burden in the cold rain. I can't help but wonder at the old man's pain.

❧ *OH COME ALL YE FAITHFUL*

This is a simple request for all those who do not know the Lord. Come because there is a reason to rejoice. We have a Savior. We have a risen Savior. This is the season to rejoice. We rejoice not only because of material gifts. We rejoice because of the spiritual gift that has been granted us.

Come and adore Him, born the King of Angels. Isaiah 9:6-7 states "For unto us a child is born, unto us a child is given, and the government shall be upon His shoulder and His name shall be called Wonderful, Counselor, The Mighty God, The Everlasting Father the Prince of Peace."

Through this child the finite becomes infinite; Hate is turned into love, war is turned to a spiritual dialogue where those who oppose each other can find common ground. But more important confusion is turned into a guiding light that will shine forever.

Come to, tomorrow and forever. Because Christ came those who accept Him will live forever. For as in Adam all die, even so in Christ shall all be made alive. I Cor. 15:22.

Merry Christmas.

GOOD-BY YESTERDAY —
GOOD MORNING SUNSHINE

The day has ended. Exhausted from laborious task. I lay me down to rest, my soul then seeks harmony with its creator. Good-by yesterday. We hold onto thy memories. Good and undesirable though they remain the past we cannot regain. A fleeting memory of which can never be again.

Good morning sunshine for with you comes revitalization. The downtrodden are drawn to your vibrant rays. With each dawn new hope arises with each sunset the cycle of time continues on. Yesterday is forever gone.

✿ I'M HERE FOR YOU

I know you're alone and you think you can't go on another day. You've lost your way and you're confused about what to do but I have just one thing to say. I'm here for you, to help you get through another day to find your way, take you by the hand and help you understand that together we can make it.

Life is so strange. You're up today and down the same. Money and friends are distant and few. But I don't want you to worry because I'm here for you.

I'm here for you. When it's cold and the road seems long. Hold on to me and I'll make you strong. If you can just hold on just a little while longer, we can pray together so we can stay together. We can weather any storm. I'm here for you.

∽ ALL THIS TIME

I see you every day as we go our separate ways. It never crossed my mind that I would find someone who would share kindred feelings and give way to reason, this I found when I found you.

All this time I thought I knew. All this time I could not see through the fog of pain we remain as though time was just a dream in my mind. I had hoped for and wished for the door that would open when I turned the key that opened to a whole new world.

All this time I wasted life that should have been tasted and savor the love that only comes once in a lifetime.

ᴥ A PEBBLE ON THE BEACH

So vast the shore upon which I lie but I'm well in reach. To gaze at my significance is bliss, I'm not a pebble on the beach.

Innumerable are we who lie upon the shore. Waves challenge nature's purpose to stand against corrosion; plan to wash away earth's soil. We're anchored in the sand.

Life offers many a challenge when one seems to stand alone. Heaven and earth seem to tremble as the saints weep and moan. Evil seems to triumph but is detained for one dares to teach. Don't be dismayed at evil's presence, be a pebble on the beach.

One is the foundation upon which others stand, for from one simple pebble this shore began. Quests come from those who dare to dream. Dreams are never out of reach. Stand for you don't stand alone. Be a pebble on the beach.

಄ WHY

I saw my father bend beneath the weight of injustice. I saw my dad cringe from the heat of indifference and I asked why?

I saw my mother shiver from the winds of segregation. I saw her walk the dirty streets of servitude with tears in her eyes and I asked why?

I saw little children huddled surrounded by the thorns of hatred and bigotry, grasping for the rose of acceptance that was overshadowed by the leaves of bureaucratic bungling and I asked why?

Then the answer came out of the pondering of my thoughts. You have the power of prayer and you have the light that will ignite the fire of freedom inside you, to let you know that I am always with you.

಄ OFF THE TOP

When anger gives way to reason. When rationality precedes emotional frenzy. When chaos becomes a placid organization. When thoughtlessness becomes careful cogitations. Then the process of peace will become attainable.

∾ *TOO MUCH*

Help me be holy. Help me be holy thine. My soul is willing but my flesh is weak, oh won't you help me be holy thine.

Help me to cling to the good. Help me to do the things I should. My soul is willing but my flesh is weak, oh won't you help me be holy thine.

There's too much stealing, and there's too much killing: There's too much taking and not enough forsaking: There's too much lying and to much denying. We all stand to lose oh my.

Help us to submit when we are wrong. Teach us that we all belong. A head with no face: There's just the human race oh won't you help us be holy thine.

⌇ IT'S OVER

Time and time again you tried. You did your best your conscience was your guide. You've stood alone, you've carried on, now it's over.

Blood, sweat, and tears you gave. Hope for the weak you often saved. Those lost and alone when all hope was gone. Ignored you for us you died. Your work is done and the victory's won. It's over.

There comes a time when we must go on. Life hasn't ended it's just begun. Don't give up or despair, life is certain it's not always fair. But now it's over.

Those tears of pain become tears of joy. You'll find your way despite the ploys. You are wiser and stronger, you don't have to take it any longer. It's over.

❧ *DEAR HEAVENLY FATHER*

Dear heavenly father. We call upon your name. What's going on in the world is just a shame. There are people on the street with nothing to eat everywhere. People are dying and people are crying we need you.

Dear heavenly father please hold our hand. We need your wisdom help us to understand. How to love. How to share, when someone's hurting how to care. Hold our hand.

We live in a world of doom and gloom. There's plenty of space but not enough room. We reach out but we're turned away. That's why we get on our knees and pray.

Heavenly father include us in your master plan. The world can't help us but you can. Give us a reason to live. Show us the way to give we need you.

༄ HE KEEPS ON BLESSING

I'm amazed at you Lord. The things you say and do Lord. We don't deserve your love. You give our daily bread. Food to eat and a roof over our head. You gave us water to drink, and a mind to think; legs to walk and a tongue to talk. You keep on blessing.

When I'm down it's not for long. Your grace goes on and on. When my enemies look for me to fall all I have to do is call. He keeps on blessing.

They said I couldn't make it. They said I couldn't take it. I don't have what it takes to see it through. I tried to fake it I just could not forsake it. His grace and his spirit is there for you too. He keeps on blessing.

ᔆ *HOW LONG*

*We cross paths every day. We don't converse anymore
we go our separate ways. It's time to stop and look
around. It's time to stand our ground. How long.*

*It doesn't look like the same town. It seems as though
we're on a merry-go-round. We can't walk the streets
we're afraid of those we meet. Something is terribly
wrong.*
                    How long.

*How long will we allow others to rule our mind. We
cling to their lies and see the world through their eyes.
How long.*

*We are slow and so unwise to heed the call of bogus
cries. We waste our time. What's yours is not mine. We
can all sing the victor's song. How long.*

31

❧ HONOR AND GLORY

We adore you. We love and behold your grace. Your mercy surrounds us we are astounded, we long to see your face.

Honor and glory to our God. The King of Kings of Kings of who the ancients sing, and angels tell of his story.

From majesty to disdain. Into a world of darkness he came to lead us to that Promised Land.

Honor and glory the elders sing and the heavens ring with echoes of power forever thou shalt reign.

❧ A NATIONAL TRAGEDY —
THE MYTH OF FREEDOM

Ode to those who dare to be free. Freedom is not secured by locality. Whether north, south, east, or west, from tyranny there is no rest.

The message is often subtle and one is foolish not to see, that the myth of freedom is a national tragedy.

In chains raped of national pride. We roamed the slopes of chastity with no place to hide. Slave ships tried to muzzle what the oceans decree the fate of a people became a national tragedy.

Drawn to the bright lights, fleeing fields of sugar cane. We fell victim to mines of ore and subway trains. Afraid of those whom we don't know and of those we can't see. It's the myth of freedom. It's a human tragedy.

32

❧ *YOU DON'T KNOW WHAT HE MEANS TO ME*

I've been down and out.
I've been all alone.
I've been so depressed I didn't think I could go on.
He was my comforter and He was my friend.
You don't know what Jesus means to me.

He's been my anchor in the roughest storm.
He's my protector.
He keeps me in His arms.
You don't know what the Lord means to me.

You don't know what He means to me.
From bondage He set me free.
He saved my soul and He made me whole.
You don't know what He means to me.

🙋 *THROUGH THE EYES OF A CHILD*

I see castles in the sky.
I see rainbows way up high.
I see angels all around.
I see fireflies as they light up the ground.
Visions of children from other lands,
The hate and confusion they don't understand.
The world seems bleak but you will learn to smile
When you view the world through the eyes of a child.

Children fight but only to amend.
For today's foe is tomorrow's friend.
We all hunger, thirst, and we all bleed.
We all suffer from hatred and greed.
Come and think and sit awhile
And view the world through the eyes of a child.

FOOTSTEPS

They seem to tell a tale that cannot be silenced.
Whether at dawn, midday or evening
They sing a song that cannot be kept
If we listen to the sound of footsteps.

Some are loud and some are quiet.
Some sneak around corners so don't deny it.
You can't cover nor are secrets kept.
The truth will give way to footsteps.

TWILIGHT

Toiling in the morning sun.
Man's fate has just begun.
Men toil to the task that's finite.
He longs to twilight.

We dream dreams of what we hope will be.
We try to change the wrong we see.
We give way to labor.
Pain of body from muscles so tight.
We long for stratums comfort
That only comes at twilight.

❧ AUTOMATION

Freeways bulging from overcrowded roads.
Big wheels bowing beneath the heavy loads.
Sirens scream in desperation all because of automation.

Cars like ants line up in pairs.
People are behind the wheel in their easy chairs.
Staring at roadside signs headed for their destination.
All made possible by automation.

Vibrations from trains quake the ground.
Shock waves can be heard from miles around.
Carrying goods to hungry nations.
All because of automation.

We'd be in total darkness.
The intense heat and cold we could not bear.
To knock progress is not fair.
Machines can also clean the air.

You can't even go on a vacation without considering
  automation.

❧ *WAR*

Battle cries, stares of fatigue, and garrisons
Brought to their knees.
Negotiations too distant and too far
Brought on because of war.

Buildings and skyscrapers that once stood tall
Are soon in ruin at war's call.
We die, we bleed ,we must concede
That war is merely aimless greed.

Finances for destruction soar stories high.
For human construction we beg and cry.
Man's annihilation is not that far.
Our fate is sealed all through war.

❧ THE CHURCH

Steeples piercing through the sky.
Tis an answer to those who ask why?
Supplying laughter and food for the soul.
The church triumphant stands brave and bold.

She has sheltered succulent in time of storm.
She's kept the wayward dry and warm.
For those in flight from evil's reign.
She gave them comfort and eased their pain.

Many a warning has come from her door.
The church for so many means so much more.
Fire and brimstone, hell and scorn have caused many
  to repent,

Be forearmed and forewarned.
What stands most essential to her earthly call is
Salvation's message to one and all.
Accept the savior it's eternal life or eternal doom.
In heaven or hell there's plenty of room.
Man can find rest from his endless search.
The answer lies with the church.

❧ LOVE WILL SHINE

Though it seems dark and dreary.
Love will shine through.
Like a knight in shining armor,
Love will emerge as a sunrise
To conquer the abysmal darkness.

Turbulent storms beat upon the frail structures of life
Only to expose the need for reconstruction.
If the rains of adversity never beat upon one's life,
The rays of the sun would never heal the wounds
Of disappointment and remind us that when there's pain,
He will be there to comfort us.

The dungeons of despair may be dark and cumbersome.
We stumble as we try to find our way.
Just hold onto whatever you do.
Just remember love will shine through.

MY DAD

Cold hands from winter's bite.
He would comfort me on those dreary nights.
Cheer me when I was sad.
That's my hero. That's my Dad.

Sometimes I think he's Superman.
Those who criticize don't understand.
He's kind, loving, brave and bold.
My dad has a heart of gold.
He works hard that I might enjoy
The pleasure of having a Christmas toy.

Life is strange and takes many a turn.
To watch your dad is a good place to learn.
To work, to play, to laugh, to cry,
To succeed, to fail, to stumble, to try.
Stand when others would pull you down.
To be a man, to stand your ground.

To some he's weird, strange,
When I see him, I get glad.
That's no bum, that's my Dad.

EMERGING

The cocoon of the butterfly.
The anguish of a baby's cry,
Leads us to know we are emerging.

The flutter of an eagle's wings.
The miracle of all living things,
Exclaim that we are emerging.

From love's quest to fulfill the empty soul
To a just and noble goal,
To the mystery that the universe unfolds,
We are emerging.

From knowledge to emotion:
From logic to the spiritual.
We act upon our feelings.
We ponder from that we think we know.
Only to refrain from an arrogant state of morbidity.
We then withdraw into a childish state.
We emanate into playful surges,
Only to learn that we have yet to emerge
Into a growing thinking, rational creature.

✌ *THIS IS YOUR TIME*

Tomorrow is not promised.
We live from day to day.
One must savor each moment
From wisdom do not stray.
Be ever so vigilant.
Always be kind.
Tomorrow for you may be today.
This is your time.

We can plan for years on what we might do.
Only God knows what the future holds for you.
Don't waste your energy.
Don't waste your prime.
Tomorrow is not promised.
This is your time.

❧ *THE MAGIC CITY*

Long ago there was a plan.
The plan helped people band.
Every creed came to understand
How to treat one's fellow man.
We welcome you to the magic city.

Voices ring from cloistered walls.
Steeples reach out to one and all.
Southern belles are awful giddy.
They're a part of the welcome committee.
Home grown in the magic city.

There's a mystic about this place.
It goes beyond one's gender and race.
They grow them wise and strong.
The heart of Dixie is where you belong.
We want your strength and not your pity.
Come on home to the magic city.

❧ COME INTO MY LIFE

Come into my life:
Come into my heart.
Come into my mind.
Satan get behind me.
Lord I need your Holy power.
I'm in a wilderness.
I need to drink from the fountain that never runs dry.
My soul is hungry for the bread of life.
My enemies may surround me.
Thank God you found me.
Lord my life is yours forever.

Come into my life.
Come into my heart.
Come into my soul.
Lord take control.
I need your holy power.

Lord help me to be a light on the hill.
Show me the way and I'll do your will.
There may be darkness but you are the light.
When everything goes wrong you'll make it all right.

❧ ONE OF THESE DAYS I'M GOING HOME

This world can be dark and cold. People can be so bold. So much hate and despair; Not much hope anywhere. One of these days I'm going home.

Hearts broken both young and old. Selling their souls for the silver and gold. In this their souls find no rest. Oh how they roam. But one of these days I'm going home.

Jesus loves me for me He died. Heaven's gate is open wide. I love the Lord He pitted every groan. One of these days I'm going home.

No more sickness. No more war, get your house in order the end is at the door. Don't ever fear for you're never alone. One of these days I'm going home.

Don't you want to go with me. I'll show you a mystery. When he comes again, to take away the pain. We'll be changed. In a moment in the twinkling of an eye. Never again will we roam. One of these days we're coming home.

❧ BE ALL THAT YOU CAN BE

If you can't be a flower with the fragrance of spring, be a sparrow in the meadow and let your voice ring. If you can't be a cloud be a tree. Provide some comfort with your shade for those who face adversity. If you can't be an ocean be a stream. Providing flowing words of support to those who would dare to dream. If you can't be a road be a trail and lead souls to that eternal well. You will not be judged by what man might decree, but for being the best that you can be.

ᔥ GOD HAS A HEART

The universe is a mystery. It has no prelude nor end.
The stars, moon, and the sun were made with passion.
God conceives again and again.

The protons, electrons, neutrons, and matter of all that
exist, and the soul of the earth that ascends from a simple
mist. All too wonderful for my reasoning, his grace he
does impart. Galaxies and worlds unknown proclaim that
God has a heart.

With tender loving care he fashioned every creature.
One marvels at each intricate detail and their unique
feature. Hence man his prized creation it's truly a work of
art. Our attributes and our capacity to love attest that God
has a heart.

Therefore the most profound display of compassion
was portrayed on the cross. His son bled and died for the
brokenhearted and the lost. The occasion on which He
wept should keep us from falling apart. It disposes what
eternity exclaims. God has a heart.

✎ FAITHFULLY YOURS

True love comes only once in a lifetime. This love should last forever. Don't let it slip away. We may never have this chance again. This day we become more than friends. It's you and me. It's our destiny. Life's shown us how we should live. For as long as we give. I'm faithfully yours.

No one will tear us apart. I give you my heart, unselfishly. This time dreams become reality. If you hold onto this vow and don't allow doubt to sway our feelings. Come what may I'm here to stay, I'm faithfully yours.

Faithfully yours; to have and to hold. Faithfully yours, my heart and soul I give to you. I'll share my dreams I'll share with you. Stand beside you in all you do. Come what may, I'm here to stay. I'm faithfully yours.

With you I can weather any storm. When it's cold I'll keep you warm. I'll keep you safe and far from harm. I'm faithfully yours.

✥ KINDRED SPIRITS

So much in common we have so much to share. In a world that has made us so unwelcomed we must beware of the pitfalls that so easily beset us as we travel through time. Kindred spirits are we, partakers of discomfort so benign.

Of laughter we smile but deep within our souls we long for the day when peace will begin so give way and joy will arrive and we will bask in the morning sun and with our lips taste the pure summer's rain. But we will not fear autumn's flora. We are dearest for we are kindred spirits.

Clones we are for the goal is the prize of eternity. Our quest for truth is an eternal flame that swelters in heartless corridors of paths unknown. We must heed the call of providence and revere it because we are kindred spirits.

❧ SOUNDS OF THE STREET

I hear sirens scream with urgency. I hear the rumbling of streetcars as they impose their will upon the winds that are filled with the repulsive stench of urban exhaustion.

Shadows flee from the glare of the noonday sun. Faces rarely meet. Fear reigns supreme. They give way to the sounds of the streets.

I attend to the traffic lights which refrain for a moment from the madness of self genocide. The deploring sound of grieving victims of a callous and indifferent society. One cannot retreat from the sound of the street.

But alas a stranger of whose origin one cannot ascertain. His feet clothed with humility. He walks softly but carries with him the message of peace. Each step echoes a plea for attention. Each stride a pronouncement of dedication to his call. Neon signs beckon. The hungry with all you can eat. A common but familiar sound of the street.

I hear boom boxes, the pulse of the hood. Here whatever you want can be found. Remnants of poison strewn on the ground. The same message just a different beat. Listen to the sound of the street.

We are in cadence with the drummer we just march to a different beat. There is a message on every corner, listen to the sounds of the street.

✎ BLOSSOM WHERE YOU ARE

A meadow of choices each to its own domain. There are apple, peach, pear, orange, and grapes all nestled in the plain.

Each bloom with a familiar fragrance that one can savor from afar. They need not impose on one another, they just blossom where they are.

We too are likened to fruit trees different but equal to its goal. Although they differ, they provide nourishment for the soul.
There are those who might prefer one taste. Another may desire a different kind. Don't worry if you're not chosen. Just be patient you will be in time.

Give yourself space to blossom. Spring into time and grow. Fruit harvested too early is sour and too hard to consume. Give way to wisdom and glow.

A flower fully blossomed adds decor from afar. Don't worry about your surroundings. Just blossom where you are.

❧ SOUNDS OF A DISTANT DRUM

Echoes travel near and far. They carry a message to and from. Sounds of love, joy, peace, and even war. They are the sounds of distant drums.

A mighty people lie deep in a continent's heart. A people warmed by a soothing sun. Nestled near the river's edge. Never afraid of what they heard or what was said. Pagan sounds to others but a language to some. The natives relish the sounds of those distant drums.

They tell of laughter; they witness to wealth. They give evidence to the truth: They dispose of death.

Mighty warriors of every clan. The right of passage they command. Men and boys attend and soon succumb to the rhythm and mystic power of a recurrent distant drum.

They come from afar to take us away to lands unknown where we are forced to obey the cruel hand of tyranny until we become, clones of servitude; ruled by the sounds of a distant drum.

☙ ALABAMA IN THE SPRING

Autumn leaves assemble and overspread the terrain, as the clouds have their winter's fling.

Nightfall casts its timely spell upon creatures large and small. They scurry to their niche eluding winter's hostile sting. Slumbering patiently for Alabama in the spring.

When alas! There's a sign of new life. Foliage sprouts with laughter as birds in majestic harmony sing.

Life is beautiful as the clear blue streams concede: It's Alabama in the spring.

☙ WORDS OF ENCOURAGEMENT

Gal. 6:2 "Bear ye one another's burdens, and so fulfill the Law of Christ." We need to help carry the load. Don't withhold a compliment when it's warranted. That was a good job you did. At the pace you're going you're going to really shine in this post.

Instead of tearing one another down, hold each other up. We all have a cross to bear. If Jesus was God and man and Simon was commanded to help carry the cross of Jesus, there are some crosses that we need help with.

We need to support one another prayerfully, financially, and lovingly. Whatever we do let it be done in love.

❧ *IS ANYTHING TOO HARD FOR GOD?*

We ponder at the amoeba, we gaze at the beauty of the stars. We travel the mighty oceans and seas, we've sent satellites to Mars.

As we read His holy word of what Moses did with his rod, it should not be beyond human reason that nothing is too hard for God.

When His children were in the wilderness they became thirsty and looked for water day after day. Their feet ached and their tongues were scorched from the sun's rays. But Moses prayed and water gushed out from a rock when He gave a nod. Then the people believed and fell to their knees. No, nothing is too hard for God.

❧ BLACK SATIN

Woven as silk ebony eyes that shine like emeralds. Sable coils of hair soft as velvet. An ageless display of women and men formed into black satin.

Skin that would break with a simple touch. Centuries have passed but we don't ask for much. The poison of oppression only made us strong. We became immune to society's wrong. When others moved out we moved in and became black satin.

A diamond in the rough whose true value is known. From our sweat and tears nations were born. Perhaps this is why we're so thicked skinned. Hearts of gold; black satin.

Spirits broken from such a waste. Lives wasted because of habitual taste. When others say we're finished that's when we begin. A specimen of God: Black satin.

❧ POVERTY'S CHILDREN

My hands are warmed by a potbellied stove. We fetch our water from a stream at Widow's Cove. My clothes are tattered, patched and re-styled. I have dreams too. I'm poverty's child.

I'm proud, too proud to beg for a morsel of bread. When it rains I can't afford an umbrella nor a cap for my head. Through all the pain I can manage a smile. Grin and bear it, I'm poverty's child.

My playmates are strays. They come from the alleys and cracks in the wall. While I cry from hunger, weapons are stockpiled. This is why I'm poverty's child.

I believe in God more than I do you. I will rise from this dunghill if it's the last thing that I do. His love will shine through if I can hold on a while. God does not care that I'm poverty's child.

❧ WALK THROUGH THE FIRE

Drawn by the warmth of desire. Passion lures us to the fire. Unscathed by warning from the flames, we dare to play a demonic game.

Walk through the flames that challenge our will. Walk through the fumes and be faithful still.

As the flames soar higher and higher with love and hope gallantly walk through the fire.

Igniting temptation trying the young and old. Shaping spirits pure as gold.

The flames singe the chaff that weighs us down, when we are tried we shall receive a crown.

Heaven's council does require to be tried, walk through the fire.

✒ *CHICAGO*

Big city dreams, small town ways. People come from near and far, they all have something to say.

Chicago, what a town.

I heard you're warm. I heard you're cold. Some say it's true others say it ain't so. Chicago, what a town.

Grant Park's the doorway to the city's heart. This is the place where so many got their start. The northside is the businessman's hide-a-way. Skyscrapers can't block the sun this ain't no city by the bay.

Chicago, what a town.

When east meets west there will be laughter in the street. There's gourmet food and the air is sweet.

Chicago what a town.

❧ *I KNOW*

I know that you've been trying.
I know that you've been crying for so long.
I know that your heart's been broken.
I know that words unspoken
Won't ease the pain of your broken heart.

I see you pass by my way but there's not a day
That I don't pray that you will overcome.
He will come along so stay strong.
He will help you along.
He knows your deep desires.
He knows you were once inspired to go on.

I know, I know, I know but don't you know
I heard every groan.
You were never alone.
I know.

ᕫ THE SNAKE IS NOT DEAD

Moored in the garden subtly to deceive,
God's prize creation Adam and Eve.
With half truths, and a smile he caused
This holy couple to lose their place,
He reduced to finite existence the whole human race.

Banished from paradise briars
And thorns became their stead
Take heed and be watchful,
The snake is not dead.
He comes as an angel of light
So be watchful as you pass.

He has camouflaged his evil ways.
There's a snake in the grass.
Lucifer, that old Satan.
The devil is as strong as he is wily.
He is as deadly as poison, and a liar.
He will kill you with a smile.

To those who doubt his eternal existence,
God's word has plainly said.
Thy soul be on thy guard for the snake is not dead.

❧ YOU DON'T HAVE TO SAY A WORD

I can tell by your smile you want to stay with me.
The touch of your hand lingers long and gently.
You don't have to say a word.

The way you move asserts your feelings.
Through static I can feel vibrations of an overzealous
   heart.
You just want to be near and your love calms all my fears.
Your thoughts are heard.
You don't have to say a word.

Silence, words never spoken,
Creates passion that lies dormant deep inside.
Motions that signal a willing spirit aimed at a heart
That should not fear it.

Love that is freely given lends itself to affection.
Preferred actions speak louder than disemblance.
You don't have to say a word.

❧ THE ROAD

Winding, bending and swerving into what seems an endless
   destination,
Signs forecast what lies ahead as well as what's foregone.
Potholes and craters irritate those who travel on the road.

Time sets no precedence on this bearing.
From sunrise to sunset wayfarers convert their way towards
   their destination.
Heavy loads travel the road.

The cracks tell of pressure placed upon its plane.
Invasion of its ingress causes it to sustain the force
Of conveyance wearing machines from hostile climates
Corrode traveling down that familiar road.

When finally it appears those who roam this popular path
Arrive at their abode.
One would never arrive had it not been for the road.

ᕙ PAIN

It hurts.
I grasp for air.
The demeanor, the mood swings are from disdain.
It's pain.

Broken promises are piercing arrows of despair
That wound the soul . . .
The letter did not come.
The raise became a figment of desire
Disconcerted by those once admired.

Decaying teeth that were once ivory towers ache.
Rheumatism induces moans that annoy companions
At all nightly hours.
Weak from a hard day's work.
Strength one tries to regain from pain.

✎ FEELINGS

I read you like a book.
Every muscle like pages leaped towards me with passion.
I could tell that you were in need of attention.

I listened with mechanical intensity,
Committing to memory every sacred word
As if they came from a dying prophet.

Then as sounds raced towards my direction
As thunder from a turbulent storm.
I withdrew for a moment to protect my feelings
From the typhoon of verbal desecration.

Composed I resigned myself to tranquil thoughts.
Comely as a master approaches his adversary for battle,
I cautiously converged upon my counterpart with
utterances of wisdom.

If I neglected to praise you: If I abandoned your
*   emotions:*
If I was preoccupied with the mundane,
Give yourself to providence and not chance.
Reconcile.

They tell of laughter. They make us rejoice with their sonnets. Humorists bring hope and uplift the downhearted. Of love that cannot be uttered from lack of expression and those too tiring to show it. Feelings scope for reprieve that comes from a poet.

They imply the way to peace. Sonneteers deplore acts of war. Human encounters are of passion concerned of situations so bizarre.

Persons of rhyme in detail describe those who have failed and of those who succeed. They tell of the pitfalls of vice and greed. They bear witness of nature's fury. Rhymers savor the gentle fragrant breezes of spring. Of heroes striking liberty's bell and shouting let freedom ring.

Rhyming of those who grace this world through the miracle of birth. Troubadours of those who descend to mother earth. The answer to life's mysteries is commonplace to those who know it. It is of poetry and prose that comes from the poet.

❧ LIGHT IN THE WINDOW

Refractions that dispel the dread of night.
Alluring the confused to a path that is right.
Though miles away it provokes curiosity from its glow.
There is a light in the window.

From dusk until dawn thoughts give way to an analytical
*   mind.*
A body submits to the weight of cogitation.
Driven by desire and thirst for wisdom to others bestow
There is a light in the window.

Alas a solution is found.
The answer will astound those who slumber and submit
*   to defeat.*
Victory comes from wisdom's mighty blow,
All from a light in the window.

❧ GEORGIA PINE

Forever towering towards heights unknown.
Displaying evergreen splendor and delicate cones.
Piercing vapors of urban slime.
One is amazed at the Georgia pine.
Determined extension despite opposition.
This evergreen is never in remission.
Always expanding, determined to shine.
There is a mystery to this Georgia pine.
Set your goals high as you grow.
You'll be amazed at the crowds and admirers below.
Be rugged, soaring timber from celestial design.
Sparkling endlessly towards greatness like a Georgia pine.

A NORTHERN RHAPSODY

Northern lights cast their shadow as they spring from falling snow. Night owls and snow bunnies disappear into their private worlds. Their footprints are a fleeting memory that few can see, as the wild sing a northern rhapsody.

Cars sputter along icy streets. Bodies shake from winter's cold. Indifferent winds crack their frostbiting whip as the lakes freeze in silence as tales are told.

Fireplaces provide the comfort zone for children nestled and safely playing at home.

The sun sets and the moon rises. Stars light up the heavens and the air is filled with glee. There's laughter and parity as we all dance to a northern rhapsody.

❧ THE HUMAN SPIRIT

Reclined on nature's mattress, no life, motionless, no will or passion. A cold damp corpse.

With a gentle whisper fire wove its way into finiteness and ignited an eternal flame, power that will never quit, thus began the human spirit.

The face of the earth may frown with cogitation. The voice of spring may wail with the ill winds of turbulent storms. Summer's blistering rays may desiccate the dew of hope bit by bit. The human spirit remains the shade of comfort.

The ravages of war may lend despair. The triumph of discord will entice courage and spur reconstruction of the broken will.

Disease may alter one's appearance, strokes may contort, fever may simmer the conscious and render the flesh unresponsive. The host that invades this corpulary, antibodies will render harmless.

Though heartbroken from bogus affection and tears from pain decimate the will to live, rebutted from appearance inclination will remit and rise above the mundane so goes the human spirit.

✌ *YOU'LL MISS WHAT YOU HAD*

You'll never miss what you had until what you had is gone.
When you see what you thought you had
Somewhere you thought you'd left alone.

Don't take life for granted.
There's no guarantee that what you have you'll keep.
Someone is plotting while you're asleep.
Guard with care, what you sow you're going to reap.
You will long for what you had when you lose
What you had, so sad.

Don't lose your mind trying to hold onto things that fade
  away.
If it's yours to keep, keep it up and it will stay.
You can't lose what you never had,
You've got to choose you'll be glad.
You'll never miss what you never had,
Life goes on and on, and on and on.

✑ BLACKNESS

Blackness is not only afros and shoes with pointed toes. It is more than handshakes and bellyaches that come from too much mad dog wines.

Blackness is about a feeling not described or defined by society.

Black people are not disheartened or gloomy. They are for the most part subjects of an indifferent culture bent on subjugation and oppression.

Blackness is about endurance and survival in a sea of arrogance. We row against the waves of ignorance and arrogance. We sail towards the shore of freedom.

Blackness is creativity. It is love in many dimensions. We are doctors, engineers, and scientists too.

Blackness is humanity. It is the embryo of civilization and the canvas of the universe from which the rainbow of cultures derive. It is not genocidal.

I am black but comely. I am gentle and adaptive. I am a light that shines in dark corridors of despair.

HOLD ON AND SEE WHAT
THE END WILL BE

I started this journey a long time ago. I was young and excited about things I didn't know. Some said I couldn't make it. Some waited to see me fall. I believe Jesus will be with me through it all.

When I cross over from mortal to immortality. When I shed this body, he has a new one for me. We'll be changed in a moment: In the twinkling of an eye. Jesus will help us understand why.

I believe I'll hold on and see what the end will be. I believe I'll hold on and see what the end will be. Hold on . . . .

Some say the streets are paved with gold. Some say in this land we'll never grow old. There's no need for the sun. He is the morning star. Salvation is free it doesn't matter who you are.

Hold on and see what the end will be. He's never failed, he's never lied. Hold on, hold on. Keep on holding on.

❧ A SEPTEMBER SONG

The hazy days of summer and the forgotten fever of spring. The casual encounters of a long weekend with one's old but familiar friends.

Feelings that unravel from the touch of casual embraces. I wonder what went wrong. The pain is so pure when I hear that September song.

The melody stirs my memory. We met one September morning. Strangers like doves in flight. We bonded at first sight. Our spirits performed as a symphonic sunrise. We embraced and nature was in complete harmony.

They wondered how long our love would last. As eternity would prove them wrong. As we danced among the stars to a September song.

MOVE UP A LITTLE HIGHER

I'm going to move on up a little higher, move on up a little higher; move on up a little higher. I'm try'n to make heaven my home.

I must pray to get a little higher. Pray to get a little higher; pray to get a little higher. I'm try'n to make heaven my home.

Gabriel is a wait'n, sitt'n at the pearly gates. The freedom train's a coming and I don't want to be late.

I'm gonna sing just a little higher. I'm gonna sing to get a little higher. I'm gonna sing to get a little higher. I'm try'n to make heaven my home.

Chorus:
I've got to love to get a little higher. I've got to love to get a little higher. I've got to love to get a little higher. I'm try'n to make heaven my home. I'm try'n to make heaven my home.

❧ THE MONOCLE

The all-seeing eye scans the universe. The fleeting shadows disappear when as the sunlight the monocle appears.

No beginning and no ending. Perpetual in its examination all is scavenged.

Every speck as particles too small to behold are magnified. Stripped of every idiosyncrasy as we pass through inspection imperious are replaced with pure love.

He stands as a monocle. Blotting out every transgression with his blood. Never to be stained again.

Forgiven so we must forgive. Understood so we come to understand that things are not always as they appear. The monocle probes beneath the surface to awaken the good that lies dormant.

I was broken. I couldn't bear to see the sun rise. I was afraid of what the day would bring. I'd close my eyes and dream of being free. Then love came along and rescued me. I'm so happy. Look at me now.

Viewed with scorn, I blamed myself for failing. I couldn't look up I'd always face the ground.

I've found the answer. I've learned to pray. I've got myself together. I've got it going on. I can face a scornful world. Look at me now. I've got a new way of walking. I've got a new way of talking. I've got love in my heart. Look at me now.

✎ JOY

When I think of what the Lord has done for me I find joy. He gave me peace within. He saved my soul—and he made me whole. I'm gonna tell it. Tell it everywhere I go. I've got joy, joy, joy.

You may be wondering how can you shout for joy. When in the midst of trouble and Satan at my door. Greater is he that is in me than he that is in the world. That's why I've got joy, joy, joy.

He gives me joy when I'm lonely. Joy, joy. When I'm talked about, joy, joy. When doors are closed in my face. Joy.

✌ *THE MASSA STILL CRACKS THE WHIP*

We sing songs of freedom. We are not free. We fail to see the invisible chains and bands of tyranny. We think we've overcome. We think we've arrived on Cannan's shores when we sank the slave master's ship. But if you listen closely the massa still cracks the whip.

Delusions of splendor. Promises never kept. Feet that bleed from years of toil and we cringe as our loved ones weep. The dehumanization of slavery, the dismantling of manhood; the breeding of humans as cattle that bear no pain. The struggle still continues. Our hopes undaunted remain.

He controls our jobs through downsizing; our bodies through the cravings of his drugs. The remnants of a once royal generation have become drunkards and thugs.

Freedom without direction will never break subjection's grip. Cries from indifference fall on deaf ears for the massa still cracks his whip. Tote that barge and lift that bale are commands of a dictatorship. A beast of burden who toils in vain. The massa still cracks the whip.

℘ MAJESTIC SPLENDOR

The galaxy is a symphony. The sons of God sing as the angels arouse a celestial opera. Hallelujah, hallelujah, hallelujah, hallelujah. For the Lord God Omnipotent reigneth. The heavens cling to praise.

The planets hang as ornaments at Christmas. Diverse in color they create an oreola in the vastness of space.

The stars light the way to God's front door. Thunder as waves that beat the shore announce his arrival.

The Milky Way as a snow-covered plain created by the finger of God is a masterpiece that hangs on the walls of space. There is so much majestic splendor.

The spiral nebula is a rainbow of terrestrial wonder. Too far for man to reach rests in the hand of God.

The earth is a microcosmic paradise that spawns vegetation. This is the core of life and so much more. Such majestic splendor. Man thus resigns himself to a humble state. Submission to such an awesome force is wise and mankind must explore the mysteries of majestic splendor.

❧ ECHOES FROM THE PAST

From the present to the past we travel through time. Echoes of souls in pain linger though centuries that have gone by.

The dusty roads of southern plantations explode from the weight of wagon wheels loaded with cultural oppression.

The reins of servitude are held firmly. The moans of broken spirits hover in the air through centuries of war and despair.

Tears of the bereaved fill the trenches hollowed by fallen souls of cultural contention. These channels merge into the sea of promise. Waves echo men marching into battle.

Drummers lead the brigade headlong into harm's way. With each beat a soul falls. Echoes of warning go unheeded. War is not the answer. Only love can conquer hate. Lingers in the clouds.

I can hear children playing with makeshift toys. Sticks are used for guns. Wood poles are the thoroughbreds of their imagination.

If one listens one can hear voices echoing we shall overcome. In silence footsteps can be heard making their way towards service. The sounds are distinct. They remind us that what has been may repeat itself. How long one's present status will last depends upon adherence to the echoes from the past.

❧ *TIME*

Time is ageless.
There is no beginning or ending.
From eternity past until eternity future time marches on.
Time is the balm that has an all-inclusive remedy.
In time a broken heart will mend.
Hatred will dissipate as a vapor and
Love will rise from the ashes of hopelessness.
In time there will be rejoicing.
The bitter winds of despair will flee from the sunlight of
 opportunity
All will occur in time.

There will be silence in the Heavens.
There will be a chilling calm.
It's time.

෨ I SEE HUMANITY

I looked upon a stranger unlike myself appeared.
Different cloths, different texture of skin. His hair was
unlike my own. Many other features that reconciled more
important he is a part of humanity.

I've sailed the unknown seas to strange lands. Customs
unbeknown were thrust upon me. Should I stay or leave?
Their needs were so great that I could not believe. They
cleaved to me with questions. Some I could not conceive.
Can't you see they proclaimed, we're a part of humanity?

We may be different: We may be from different lands.
The world is so small. Countries are merely bridges that
connect human needs.

All blood is red. We all need eyes to see. We all have a
need to belong. We all desire to be free. We all have the
same creator and we don't need an apology. We demand to
be acknowledged as a member of humanity.

✑ GO ON

If you find yourself alone and it seems that no one cares,
Go on.

Though your way seems dark and dreary,
Go on.

When you lose that you hold dear, don't give way to fear.
Go on.

Ask and it shall be given; seek and ye shall find:
Knock and the door shall be opened unto you.
Go on.

Go on with your dreams: Go on with your plans.
Don't give up, go on.

❧ IT'S GONNA BE ALL RIGHT

You may be going through trials and tribulations.
Your heart may be heavy from the pain you bear.
Just lean on him and leave your burdens.
You're safe in his arms and he'll calm your every fear.

   It's gonna be all right;
   It's gonna be all right; keep holding on.

You will go through tribulations.
When you don't know what to do about your situation.
Place your cares on him and leave your troubles behind.
His yoke is easy and he will ease your mind.

✑ CHIMES

Sounds of a blessed union, assuaging to those who would
    wed.
They calm the weary soul, they bring great relief to those
    upon their sick bed.
Sounds that introduce the stranger as well as open the
door to a loved one trapped outside in winter's cold and
no key is under the mat on the floor.
Strange sounds then a chilling silence one's life in retro
    spect is read.
Chimes render life's reward and pacify the souls of the
    dead.
They still the raging winds and bitter rains of labor.
One's work we cannot refrain.
Chimes that give us hope to go again and again.
Ringing in new chapters of life.
Each gong is a page of mortal depiction.
Chimes are unique in their melodic description.
Chimes

✨ I MISS YOU SO

I opened the door only to find that you were gone.
You slipped away without saying a word.
Where did you go?
I miss you so.

It's not the same because love has gone.
It's not the same because love has died.

I no longer smell the fragrance of your gourmets.
The smell of morning provision would awaken a tired soul
Don't you know I miss you so?

Your warm smile that would greet me at the door.
Arms ready to console always inquiring what's wrong.
Silence grips the air that you once invaded with words of
    wisdom.

Echoes of counsel are embedded in my mind.
You'll never be forgotten.
I miss you so.

❧ *PARADISE*

A far away place to those who would dare to dream.
A place of tranquility still and serene.
Hidden from those who obscure peace and are torn
  with hate
Will never realize heaven's gate that leads to paradise.
Many who seek it fail to discover
It cannot be bought or found in a lover.
It is eternal and so peaceful and surrounded by stars.
There is nothing uncommon nor bizarre.
Paradise is a philosophy that lies within.
It's a place of love that transcends race and gender.
Mankind must surrender himself to truth in order
To realize that we hold the key to paradise.

❧ THE ROSE

Delicate, beautiful, rare.
It stands alone.
Distinctive, fragile, protected
By thorns from those who would violate its domain:
Nature in prose depicts the rose.

It is a symbol of endurance;
The rose has withstood the test of time.
Its petals symbolize gentleness.
They remind us to be unhurried to all that pass by.
To take courage at adversity.
One only falls to rise again.

A symbol of quiet strength.
When it is given hearts are transformed.
Passion melts hearts of stone.
Love presides because of the rose.

✎ *DEATH*

Death is the transition from finiteness to eternity.
It is a path that all must travel.
He is that dreaded adversary of life.
He is eminent in his destination.
He is never late.
When he arrives it is one's time to depart.

Death is the destroyer that comes in diversity.
Without consideration of grief.
His task is carried out with precision.
Death is that dreaded stranger:
A companion of darkness.

To those without hope he is a welcome guest.
He does not stay long.
To those who are consumed with pain
He is the balm of Gilead.
Those who have eternity's promise see him
Merely as a prelude to infinity.

THE ARTIST OF MY SOUL

Carefully painting a picture of how I should be.
Forming me so tenderly as I grow through pain and
* suffering.*
With each stroke of care you teach me to be brave
In trials and adversity without losing my way
In a world that's cold.
You're the artist of my soul.

Sketching my character with disappointment.
Depicting courage with adversity.
Becoming strong and bold.
Learning to appreciate beauty from the unlovely
From the artist of my soul.

❧ THE SEASONS OF LIFE

Mainspring is a time of innocence. This is a period of total dependency. There are cries from necessity but they are silenced by spiritual and physical nutriment.

One's existence depends upon one's caretakers. One is defenseless, one is deprived of the tools that one needs to sustain one's life. Growth occurs as the rays of awakening pierce the shadows of ease. Hence one emerges into a tower of good or evil.

Clothed with will, might and youth, the challengers of summer are vaporized as untimely rain on a hot summer's day.

The fall of life quickens the descending leaves of time. Declining hair becomes a combatant of vigor. One begins to lose one's step, the quickness of wit, and wrinkles appear as streaks of white clouds on a midday blue sky.

Death comes as an untimely ice storm. It brings chills and despair to those bereaved.
For those that remain it instills a sobering reality. Nothing in this sphere lasts forever.

It is imperative seedlings demise. Fruit is replenished from their passing. Thus man must die in order to gain another spiritual dimension. Thus are the seasons of life.

❧ FOREVER YOURS

Forever I promise to love you. I will never let you down. Come what may I make this solemn promise. I promise you I'm forever yours.

We take our vows before Heaven. The angels witness this decree. As long as there are stars in Heaven, it's gonna be you and me.

True love comes only once in a lifetime. Don't let this chance pass us by. We can't wait forever. This I promise until the day I die. I'm forever yours.

God has joined us together. On this day two become one. It's you that I love and adore. This you must always remember that I'm forever yours.